INNER LIFE

OTHER BOOKS BY NOEL PEATTIE

A Cup of Sky with Donald Culross Peattie (Houghton Mifflin, 1950)
A Passage for Dissent: The Best of Sipapu, 1970–1988 (McFarland Press, 1989)
Freedom to Lie: A Debate about Democracy with John Swan (McFarland Press, 1989)
Amy Rose: A Novel (Regent Press, 1995)
Western Skyline (Regent Press, 1995)
Hydra & Kraken or, the Lore and the Lure of Lake-Monsters and Sea-Serpents (Regent Press, 1996)
In the Dome of St. Laurence Meteor (Regent Press, 1999)
King Humble's Grave (Regent Press, 2001)
Sweetwater Ranch (Regent Press, 2002)
The Testimony of Doves (Regent Press, 2005)
Inner Life: The Politics of Daydreaming (Regent Press, 2005)

INNER LIFE

Or,

The Politics of Daydreaming

(with notes from the dreamer)

by

Noel Peattie

ISBN: 1-58790-113-7

Library of Congress Control Number: 2005920132

Regent Press
6020 – A Adeline Street
Oakland, California 94608
www.regentpress.net

"But these still remain: the quietness of dawn,
and the furtive fall of night."
— Max Picard, *The World of Silence*

Contents

Inner Life

Theme Stated

Rosalie demanded of me, in the course of an argument, "What kind of society do you want, anyhow?" Over some twenty years this irritant has worked on me almost every day. The answer I propose is: that the society I desire, and which, on a universalizing principle, I want for all, is a society which protects, promotes, and honors the inner life.

The mourning dove, in the November clearing fog.

I would further suggest that the demands — heard from pole to pole, for freedom, justice, security, equality, education, a safe environment, and a better life for the world's children — are all grounded in, and reach downward to, this elemental human need: silence, solitude, and the right to rule one's own thoughts: the sanity of the inner life.

And finally: this inner life, I contend, is an endangered species: assaulted without, and subject to disease within.

What Is the Inner Life?

The term is not found in the thesaurus of the American Psychological Association; it finds no place in the *New Catholic Encyclopedia*; it is not mentioned in the four-volume *Encyclopedia of Psychology*, nor in *The Oxford Companion to the Mind*. The Library of Congress does not list such a subject heading, although there is one for SOLITUDE. Exploring reference books in psychology will lead you to such topics as "consciousness," "the mind-body problem," "personal identity," "creativity," and so forth; but what I mean by the inner life includes, and is more than, all of these.

Nor is it the same as "Inner Light," generally taken as the central belief or concern of the Society of Friends. George Fox, founder of the Quakers, is very clear on the nature of the Inner Light. He says it is a created, not natural, light (*Journal*, ed. Nickalls, p. 471). Elsewhere he identifies it with the Light of Christ, which lightens everyone who comes into the world (John 1:9). However, the inner life is not a divine, created light; it derives from simple consciousness, which we share with at least some of the animals. What level of intelligence — however we may define that word — is necessary for an inner life, I do not pretend to know; at the very least it would require some degree of memory; cats and dogs and horses have memory, but I would hesitate to ascribe it to a jellyfish. Never mind; what the nature of animal minds may be, I leave to the comparative psychologists. All I can perceive, is that if animals have an inner life, we cannot share it. Communication with them we sometimes do have. But not only is our possession of language, based upon the capacity for symbolic thought, a possession they lack, but our own language poses a reverse barrier, a barrier to our understanding their minds. Those animal minds are based on instinct and a few simple reactions trained by memory. Therefore, our human inner life requires some further definition: one that distinguishes it from simple consciousness.

If I am driving down the street, and a pickup truck turns in front of me, I will notice the pickup, take steps to avoid rear-ending it, and observe that it sports a bumper sticker. The sticker reads: GOD, GUTS, AND GUNS MADE AMERICA GREAT. If I simply notice the sticker, and concentrate on not hitting the truck, I am not more than conscious of it; simple consciousness is at its daily work. If I have not seen this particular bumper sticker before, I may react to it, thinking briefly, "That is a political position with which I really don't agree." I am still operating, mentally, at the level of simple human consciousness. If, however, I begin to reflect on the position thus expressed — if I associate it with other, similar positions I have read about or heard expressed verbally — if finally I say, "There is a position that I really abhor, but now I can think of a rational reply to that position, one which will convince at least some people that the position expressed by the bumper sticker is wrong" — if I then (turning the corner safely!) formulate plans to organize a campaign, write my representative in Congress, urge the Friends Committee on National Legislation to take my cause up as a Quakerly concern, and finally dream up a slogan, a logo, and a way of raising fifty thousand dollars to defeat that bumper sticker — then, Friends, I am living an inner life.

The inner life, therefore, is that world summoned up in the central theme of Yeats's wonderful poem, "Long-legged Fly." It is what makes possible divine worship, artistic creativity, scientific investigation, and yes, political activism! — even such apparently irrelevant matters as hobbies, crafts, and sports. In fact, all of us approach the inner life at least part of the time, and certainly all of us at night. Dreams — which occur in at least some animals — are an inner life, although a confused one.

In planning tomorrow's picnic, in learning a simple or complex skill, in resolving at night a problem that had eluded one during the day, — again the inner life makes itself manifest.

After long illness, the sense of returning health.

Two examples: where the inner life is not present, where it is present.

The soldier in combat has no inner life. He is conscious of the thunder of the guns, he is aware of the danger, but he has been trained to be an efficient fighting-machine; he has no time to be aware of anything but his objective, and he certainly has no time to dream or to remember. His objective is to get to the top of the hill and survive, and to kill anybody and destroy anything that stands in his way. If he makes it, well and good; if not, all dreams stop together. It is clear that war, and even peacetime military service, are not conducive to the inner life; and perhaps this is an argument for pacifism that pacifists themselves have not thought of. Imagine a young man saying to a recruiting officer, "I'm sorry, I don't want to join the army; it will give me no time to daydream."

The ordinary person who is living a rich inner life, however, is the one in love. Nearly all of us have had the experience of being in love, and the inner life thus generated is as intense as anything found in the half-forgotten play of childhood. The lover — I speak as a man — spends his time fantasizing about his beloved, thinking up little presents to give her, seeing a flowering tree and reminding himself to show it to her the next time they pass by there, hearing jokes and imagining how she would smile at them, fantasizing how he would like to kiss her or touch her in special places or special ways — enough! the inner life of the man in love has been deeply altered and intensified by his encounter. Fantasy plays a large part of it.

The inner life, then, is not just simple animal consciousness; it is not the Inner Light of Fox and the Quakers, but perhaps enables one to use that Inner Light — for if you are just drifting along, you may not be open to what that Light may be able to show you; nor is it restricted to men and women of genius. What forces or activities help the development of the inner life, and what ones hinder it? What would a society be like in which the inner life was honored, encouraged, protected, and open to anyone who wished to live it more fully? What would be the consequences of a society so dedicated: would it be a sensitive plant unable to survive the return of an Ice Age, or would it be more likely to survive than a society devoted simply to conquest and exploitation? And if we deem such a society desirable, how do we get there from here?

It Would Seem That Not...

Before going further I should try to defend the inner life against possible detractors. There are so many detractors of just about any philosophical position, now at the end of the twentieth century, the age of analysis and deconstruction, that almost everyone who celebrates anything as private, as *idios* — the Greek word for "private" — is immediately put on the defensive. The first and most obvious is that a rich inner life prevents, or could prevent, much of the world's work from getting done. The child is required to put away the toy dinosaur and attend to the business of learning to read, write, and reckon. Later the adolescent learns the amazingly complex business of learning how to drive a car — requiring considerable dexterity of hands, plus ability to judge time, speed, and distance; and perhaps she or he will also learn similar, but different skills in piloting a plane or sailing a boat. The daydreamer, the inattentive, risks at the very least an annoying mistake, at the worst the lives of himself and his passengers. The sea, the air, and the freeway are unforgiving of mistakes. "You weren't paying attention!"

Even at moments of leisure, the inner life can lead to loss of awareness of one's surroundings. "I see so little of Mr. Blake," said William Blake's wife to a neighbor; "he is always in Paradise." (The Blakes had no children). In the larger world, we are told, it is of overwhelming importance to support the strike, save the seals, ban the bomb, and boycott the bullies — for there is a time factor: the guys in the black hats are armed, numerous, and ready to take over in the next few days. So the dreamer must leave his cell and ride with the rangers, establishing justice from border to border.

Seeing pink clouds in an early spring dawn.

Indeed, one of the strongest objections to the inner life is that it has nothing to do with the quest for justice. The contemplative is simply not doing his or her share: in Central America, in East Timor, or here at home. One possible answer that could be given to this reproach is that social activism itself can preoccupy the mental energies that contribute to the inner life; like the soldier in combat, the activist is too busy to dream out the window. At all events, the quest for justice, like the search for other "absolutes": freedom, economic security, and education, is the pursuit of the right means to the inner life I am attempting to define and defend.

In a sense there's no arguing with these social imperatives. Nobody will suppose that you should fantasize on the freeway (though many do). And a complete avoidance of public participation is probably impossible to achieve. What is in question is whether the inner life is desirable at all; whether there ought to be people who are inner-directed, rather than outer-directed, and if so whether they should be encouraged or merely tolerated, like the young lover who wanders drunkenly through the blossoming groves, writing his girlfriend's name on every tree.

For some the inner life is inherently suspect: as being fraught with its own set of dangers. Much of the older religious literature on this subject is found under the heading, "Dark night of the soul." Those thinkers and poets who have undergone depression and either emerged from it (Tennyson) or never emerged alive (J. B. Phillips) are nowadays joined to those whose imaginations have been covered by temporary cloudings: not only survivors of rape and child abuse, including ritual persecution, but actual mental illness. Finally, even the healthy have been forced to the simple recognition that the imagination, tired, over-stimulated, or apprehensive, is susceptible to disease. Emily Brontë's poem, "God of Visions," describes her own imagination:

> And yet, a king, though prudence well
> Have taught thy subject to rebel.

Memory has a role to play in this disturbed imagination. A great deal of effort is consumed by families and lovers who, having absorbed, willy-nilly, the Freudian doctrine that to rehearse the past is good, rehearse its injustices endlessly. This is clearly a case in which the inner life, which ought to be the fortress of personal security and the studio of creative arts, is transformed into a savage temple, in which antique blood, like that in the phial of Saint Januarius, is liquefied from time to time to sully, not sanctify, the wretched witnesses. It would be better to be a sacrificial sheep, than to be part of such a ceremony; but this is one of the diseases to which the inner life, like every other part of the human heritage, mental or physical, is subject.

The story goes that a lady, who well knew the Duke and Duchess of Windsor, was asked by a friend, what that couple talked about in their childless evenings. "They talk about the Abdication." "Surely not every evening?" "Yes, *every* evening."

There is no question that the inner life can indeed

be corrupted, and some teachers and parents see the child playing alone as being in danger. "Go out and play with the other kids" is sometimes a very wise piece of advice; at other times it is an interference with the development of the soul's powers. For adults, "the thing to do is something" is equally wise advice.

The recent analysis of the psychological background of the man arrested as the "Unabomber" emphasized this danger in the public mind. The suspect was described largely in terms of his cluttered room at Harvard, his fascination with explosives, his strange theories (which were never explained in detail), his interest in mathematics, his abandonment of a secure teaching job at the University of California at Berkeley, and finally his removal to Lincoln, Montana (described as a remote place; actually, it's in the same county with the state capital). The subtext, for this reader, of the articles in *Time* and *Newsweek* was: If you don't make your boy clean up his room, drop that interest in math, and go out for team sports, he'll end up mailing bombs to people. The fact that, due to illness in infancy, he was deprived of family love and comfort at a critical point in his life, was mentioned only once. "His personality seemed to go flat," said *Newsweek*. Is that why he turned to package bombs? Even loners need love. But they shouldn't have to give up their psychological security to get it.

A further objection to the inner life is the egalitarian one. Nearly all the apologies for the contemplative life assume leisure: time, private space, and money for the intellectual or dreamer. For many this is held to be personally unattainable; for others it is undesirable. The worker says, "I'd love to be able to write poems; but I have no training—and no time to acquire any." The mother cries, "But I have mouths to feed!" Still others, quite reasonably, point out to us that those in this society who have the most wealth and leisure often spend it without any real effort toward an inner life; they simply accumulate more possessions, without even trying to live the life of the mind. They therefore call for a society without any leisure, other than weekends or retirement. Like the antagonist, born under Scorpio, in W. H. Auden's poem "Vespers," they want a society in which "he who dislikes work will be very sorry he was born."

Hearing any owl.
Watching any snake.

In Spite of All

The Need for an Inner Life as Reflected in the Environmental Movement

The environmental movement is perhaps the clearest public example of the deep desire for an inner life. "In wildness is the preservation of the world," wrote Thoreau, and this statement could only be made by a poet with a very deep and productive inner life. On a strictly utilitarian basis — "the greatest good of the greatest number" — the environmental movement would have no real standing. "The greatest good of the greatest number" would have us exterminate wolves, not re-introduce them to places whence they had been driven out a century ago; after all, "the greatest number" eat beef; they don't sit out on a mountain peak listening to wolf calls. The argument for the environmental movement, at least in its wilderness phase, is basically psychological and religious: an inner-life type of argument. I have never seen a wolf — I don't particularly care to meet one; I certainly don't want to be pursued by one — across a frozen lake, while huddled in a one-horse sleigh — but these eventualities are so unlikely that they don't enter into my environmental consciousness. The basic reason (for me) for re-introducing wolves into Yellowstone National Park is that if wolves are free, there is a place in my head that is free.

This attitude of mine, which many others share, possibly accounts for the some of the ire of the "wise use" movement, which seeks to log, shoot, graze, and mine, without regard to the finitude of natural resources and the fact that all land is holy land. The noise these agitators make suggests that they despise and fear anyone who has an inner life and wants, as a consequence, wilderness, solitude, and peace. The battle over sightseeing aircraft over the Grand Canyon is another example: those who have been down in the Canyon used to marvel at the great quiet down there, which has now been disrupted by fly-overs.

The argument has been made, by Gary Snyder and others, that the disease of Western civilization results from its loss of contact with wilderness, with a sense of kinship with Bear, Otter, Raven, and with a sense of a cosmic Mind overarching and nourishing everything

("Plain talk," 1969). However, people are not bears or ravens; although all are part, if you like, of the One Cosmic Mind — Gary Snyder is an internationally famous literary man, with many experiences and possibilities in his life; and Bear is simply, grandly, Bear. Snyder would reply that we ought to follow "primitive" traditions and treat bears and ravens as a kind of people. This suggestion opens great possibilities for those who, like Snyder, live in a montane forest; for those who live in more settled areas, the concept has some difficulties in implementation.

The evolution, on this planet, of a tool-making, fire-using, speaking, and eventually writing animal, was bound to disturb the wilderness purity that reigned at least up to the Pliocene. That disturber of the peace was us. We destroy even as we create, and that will be true as long as the human species lasts. Should we then accept the fact that with intelligence, evil was bound to come, and therefore cease to resist self-styled "progress"? To do this is to *wish* to be driven crazy; to make impossible the work of the free creative intelligence that is the *good* part of the human heritage. St. Paul described this as "sinning that grace may abound" and forbade it in God's name.

Moths, coming to a desert light.

Obstacles to the Inner Life

I mentioned the child who is required to put away the toy dinosaur and concentrate on the schoolroom task. No one will argue that this is wrong (except the child), but obstacles to the inner life arise not in the classroom but outside it. The daydreaming child is an object of puzzlement, contempt, or hostility when viewed by many other children. The loner is made to feel "weird." Conversely, the early development of many men and women of ability in the arts, and sometimes the sciences, is marked by a period of solitude, of forced withdrawal, often through illness or removal to a distant location, in which the child has time for introspection (protected, however, by a loving parent or two). Sometimes one other child is present, a playmate or a sibling not too far distant in age. The child who is constantly involved in team sports, interacting with other children or adults, may become more considerate of others and learn team skills and cooperation, but is less likely to become introspective or develop an inner life sufficient to bring forth latent creative possibilities. (These suggestions apply to girls as well as boys. The socialization of girls is different, no doubt, but no less intense). An extensive and sensitive discussion of these factors is given by Elise Boulding in Children and Solitude (1962; Pendle Hill pamphlet no. 125).

We are beginning to see one of the preconditions for the inner life: solitude, and the need for it, not just the occasional toleration of it that we assert as "the right to privacy." The club and the team may be essential for learning sportsmanship, cooperation, and managed competition. But what they produce is the team member, not the individual working artist or scientist.

Adolescence and early youth are the great period of socialization, even for the (formerly) solitary child. Not only because of sexual development, but because the mind, mushrooming with new ideas and interests, needs someone to share them with.

"But it was friends to die for,
That I would seek and find."

Solitude at this stage can become oppressive and frightening. Or it can become pointlessly introspective: the endlessly scribbled drawing or writing that never burgeons into anything interesting. Out of that comes the need for work, for education and training, without which, as Joyce Cary points out in *Art and Reality* (1958), the creative spirit will never produce any good art. But here is another obstacle to the inner life: the student becomes so interested in getting through school and finding a job, that the inner life is set aside. Marriage and family increase that pressure. As Cyril Connolly wrote in *Enemies of Promise* (1938): "Sometimes there is no greater enemy of art than the pram in the hall."

The sea, rounding any headland.

Or television. I strongly suggest that no one who wants a creative life, as poet, philosopher, thinker, worshipper, can afford to have the tube in the house. The literature against television is extensive, including discussions of its propensity to induce violent or disruptive behavior in children, but for our purposes the worst future of television is that it substitutes for the imagination. It does that so well, and so often with propagandistic intent not easily detected by the young and inexperienced, that it becomes pervasive, an addiction. Some children and adolescents eventually become bored with television, but for many adults it is a new and ever-attainable "virtual reality." A book you can always shut, for a time, and reflect on what you have read. The tube goes on forever, and it gives you no time to reflect. A carpenter, working on new siding for my house, which took many days, finally noticed that there is no television here and remarked, "I see you're not a believer in television." I silently noted the word *believer.*

Max Picard (another Jewish-Catholic philosopher, this time Swiss) in his book *The World of Silence* (1952; translated from *Die Welt des Schweigens*, 1948) sees the loss of silence as the loss of a divine center to the human world: in the past, words and music emerged from silence, now they emerge from noise and sink back into noise. He points out that if an antique statue of a god were to be excavated, and then begin to speak and move as a god, everyone would be silent; but then presently a truck would come and carry the god away, and then it would no longer be a god, but a curiosity, and its speech would be swallowed up in noise, which is the enemy of silence.

The Internet is another destroyer of the inner life; but it makes no noise, and calls no attention to itself, like the telephone. But even cases of computer-addiction, especially among adolescents, have been noted.

The first sight, through a telescope, of the planet Jupiter and its four great moons.

I recently joined a sailing club in a trip among the Bahamas. One of the astonishing things about this experience was the extraordinary lack of the usual urban stimulus available to the island wanderer; other than some shop signs in Man-o' War Cay, and a black lady preacher who ambled up and down the walkways of Hope Town, on Elbow Cay, shouting to everyone within earshot (which was just about the whole population, in a town that small) to praise God, for Jesus was coming, — the principal audio-visual impact was made by flocks of Zenaida doves, who flew from tree to tree, and by laughing gulls who besieged the aft-decks of any yacht they saw peopled with diners. Our skipper, an eighth-generation Bahamian, kept the radio from West Palm Beach going while we sailed from cay to cay, so that we could hear (I did not want to hear, but hear I did) the traffic conditions on the freeways in southeastern Florida. He told us that electricity only came to some of the cays in the late 1950s, and that it wasn't until the 1960s that he saw his first television. O lost blessed solitude!

Obstacles to the inner life, therefore, include much that our society applauds and encourages. The right-minded enemies of the inner life merely embody the quiet pressure of society, as palpable in Pasadena or Buffalo, as in a Polynesian tribe or a Benedictine convent. The Left, also, has its folkways, mores, customs and taboos.

The obstacles to the inner life are now so numerous that it may be necessary to take up arms against them, morally or physically, unless one can escape. If one can escape, to a mountain chalet, a desert rancho, or a tropical island, so much the better, but in war zones (like former Yugoslavia) or in busy American cities, it becomes impossible to attain the time and space for reflection. Whatever you do — whatever cause you champion — you rapidly become involved in the telephone calls and the position papers, and you find yourself surrounded by the proverbial alligators while attempting to drain the proverbial swamp.

Since what we are discussing are the conditions in which the inner life can survive, one rock-bottom condition must be peace and security, local and global. The individual should not have to worry about his — and more importantly, her — personal safety. "Good novels are written by people who are *not frightened*, "wrote George Orwell in "Inside the Whale" (1939). Later, in "The Prevention of Literature," he said, "the imagination, like certain wild animals, will not breed in captivity." Hence the reluctance of my imaginary recruit to join the army because it would give him no time to daydream. (Of course, if the recruiting officer had told him, "No, but there's plenty of time-wasting and bullshitting going on in the service," he might have joined, but recruiting officers are very well paid not to be specific).

Among the threats to the inner life is the lack of inner security posed by a long modern adolescence, in which the youth is physically ready, but not judged psychologically ready, to join the mature world. In part this isolation of the young is a legacy of economic conditions: the disappearance of free land, the increasing complexity of work and the need for education, and the need for a capitalist economy to save on labor costs by discouraging young people from entering the labor force too early.

A further obstacle is presented by the well-meaning, who assume that the solitary child is the "sick" child, who is likely to end up in the hospital for incurables if he starts playing alone or talking to himself. Solitude, a precondition for the inner life, was — in some cases perhaps still is — considered dangerous. Still later, the daydreamer, or any person quietly "staring into space," will be interrupted by another person's hand being waved in front of his face, sometimes with the admonition, "Wake up! You were daydreaming!" If this intrusion into the inner life is met with violence, the violence is perhaps well-deserved. The prevalent idea that we ought always to be up and doing, for solitary thought may lead to madness, is to be resisted.

Looking out a window at a quiet sunny garden.

Still more obstacles: the presence in one's life of the manipulative neurotic, the obsessive, righteous person, who as parent, sibling, teacher, pastor, older friend, or younger dependent, demands more share of one's attention than is healthy for one's own development. A modern term for this relationship is co-dependency; I style the oppressive person an "attention junkie." Victorian literature abounds in these types. The manipulative persona has not, of course, disappeared with the late Queen; when a body of people numbering in the hundreds are affected, we get Jim Jones in Guyana and David Koresh in Texas; when the population rises to the scores of millions, we get Hitler and Mussolini.

The later years bring other obstacles to the inner life that are not often expected by the young. Much of the conversation of older people, they may have noticed (if they have any patience to listen to it, and I for one can't blame them if they don't), consists of what James Joyce referred to as "Aches-les-Pains." Certainly, a preoccupation with declining vigor or health, while natural enough, is an obstacle to the inner life and has to be resisted, as vigorously as we resisted parental interruptions and manipulations in youth. This time it is ourselves, and the fossil parent inside ourselves, who has to be routed. Here solitude, the tender companion of childhood, becomes as much a monster as a friend. It requires a lot of hard work to be successfully old.

Less obvious, but more pervasive, are the standards and values of one's own society. The schools, the church, the media, the armed services, and many other factors are daily placing before every citizen a model of what America should be and the steps that we are all to take to get there. We need no conspiracy theory to explain these universal practices of social control; they are possibly older than the evolution of the species *Homo sapiens*, and probably achieved their present force with the development of language and the sense of a future. In any case, it may be possible to defy, briefly, the social conventions; what is almost impossible for anyone is to think one's way completely around and outside them, and to act that way persistently and consistently.

A consequence of such defiance of social norms, even with the best of intentions, is the mind-destroying experience of failure, or fear of failure. "Nothing more unqualifies a mind to act with prudence," wrote Jonathan Swift, "than a misfortune that is attended with shame and guilt." Like disease and crime, failure and the fear of failure destroy that inner life which makes right action possible. Fortunately, in many cases, the failing person turns his or her attention to another field, and earns a modest success. Or he may even come back to the old field with renewed strength and understanding. Someone has suggested that in the lives of the most successful men and women, there lies an early history of failure or disappointment in a different, or related, field.

Repairing a damaged thing.

Revising a poem.

Defense of the Inner Life

The poet Peter Viereck, in his Pendle Hill pamphlet, Inner Liberty; The Stubborn Grit in the Machine (no. 95, 1957), gives the answer to such fears in the character of his "Unadjusted Man," saying of his creative efforts, "The test is pain. Not mere physical pain but the exultant, transcending pain of self sacrifice," and extols the "fight for the private life." Viereck's almost Nietzschean hero is defiant in his own way: Viereck insists that the nonconformists' "strongest bulwark against mob pressures is religion, if only they would cease to spurn it," and he cites, approvingly, Saint Thomas More, knight and martyr. On the other hand, he applauds the "free personality" of the amateur, and insists that only by not knowing how to write too well or how to fight a war can you possibly attain the highest literary, philosophical, or military achievements. (This thought should comfort those who suffer from apprehension, or who know themselves to be grossly incompetent, however much it may fail to reassure their readers or their front-line troops. Those are the folks who may feel the pain). Viereck, however limited his almost libertarian position may be, has one important point to make: the opposition to the inner life may be more than merely conformist, it may be harsh. Nearly every artist and thinker has something in her or his past to remember of this sort, some parent or teacher or buddy who tried to deflect the course of the stream of inner consciousness in the name of neurotic control, authoritarianism, or simple "good-fellowship." Joyce never forgave the character he named "Blazes Boylan" for trying to make him into an Irish drunk.

Howard Haines Brinton, in The Quaker Doctrine of Inward Peace (Pendle Hill pamphlet no. 44, 1964) offers a different defense of the inner life. It would not occur to him to find the best way, as an amateur, to attain high literary or military achievements; rather he seeks the inner life as a consequence of self-surrender to God. Viereck's restless striving amateur is here replaced by the Quaker forms of John Woolman, George Fox, and lesser-known figures such as Thomas Shillitoe, who found a "habitation of peace" and when faced with temptation "got atop of things."

The defense of the inner life, therefore, whenever it needs a defense, may proceed on one of two levels: the secular and the sacred: the way of the draft resister and the way of the Desert Father. In any case it is bound to fail, if for no other reason than that we all die. The visionary hopes for eternal life after death; the poet looks for at least temporary immortality through his work. Both gamblers may be losers; but: they can do no other. The important concern for us, however, is to see what kind of society may give them the greatest grounds for hope, during that short period that we call life.

A Society for the Inner Life

We have already seen that a condition of peace — stability under the rule of law — is necessary for the inner life. In the long run, such a condition would have to be planet-wide. The experience of small countries overwhelmed by dictators across the border, common enough in the twentieth century, should make that clear. How to achieve that condition, in a state of international anarchy, is not a discussible problem for most of us: it strikes too near home.

Once public order and personal security are attained — necessary conditions for any kind of society at all — we can go on to the special requirements for the society that will foster the inner life of the mind. The first area of protection should be human sexuality and the privacy of women. A society which protected the inner life would therefore have to protect, but also leave alone, all sexual activity that involved adults only, and that employed neither force nor fraud.

There is no substitute for the bedrock virtue: decency. (Curiously, this word has a different meaning in much of America: it means being properly clothed and using inoffensive language, rather than treating other people with respect and a sense of their right to dignity and privacy). Beyond the privacy of the body comes the privacy of the mind, and this begins with children of both sexes. We have already seen the importance of the private lives of children in Elise Boulding's little book, Children and Solitude. School is the primary socializing arena for children, and except in a very few country schools, there will be little chance for a child to wander away by herself or himself; the teacher will be naturally solicitous about the child's safety — what if he hurts himself, will his parents sue? After classes there are games, after school chores, supper, homework, sleep. How is the delicate plant of the inner life going to survive? The Brontës in their parsonage, poor as they were, had their mythical kingdom of Angria; at that they were luckier than many a student in a middle-class school in America today.

If it is true that the average child in America spends a large fraction of waking time watching television, then here, at least, the inner life is an endangered species. The only possible defense that parents and teachers can provide is to bestow on the child fantasy of the best kind: the Tolkien books, Hans Christian Andersen, the magical classics. The publishers would do all of us an immense service if they would bring back into print everything illustrated by Arthur Rackham and Howard Pyle, and as for the texts, they should be left as is, not dumbed down. Rackham's illustration of a small boy riding Leviathan (originally done, without the rider, for The Tempest) does more for the imagination than any number of "correct" books (this is not to deny the importance of emphasizing books which avoid racial and other stereotypes). The Japanese should be bringing out reprints of the Japanese fairy tale series, in English, published by T. Hasegawa a hundred years ago; they were double-stitched, sturdy enough, and contained most horrific goblins and giant centipedes — all defeated by heroic warriors, such as "My Lord Bag o'Rice," and the fellow who exterminated "The Ogres of Oyeyama." There were stories for girls, too, like the touching "Matsuyama Mirror." Those who disapprove of fantasy for children are hereby sentenced to read W. H. Auden's poem, "A New Age."

If there is any possibility of getting the adolescent away from a strictly peer society, even for a time, it should be pursued. The sulky boy who discovers the wisdom of his grandfather and the joys of power-boating in the film *On Golden Pond* (1981) is a beautifully illustrated case in point. Student exchange programs such as the ones administered by the American Field Service and others are also helpful. (But these are usually only open to students of outstanding achievement.) The issue is not simply one of safeguarding the kids from drugs and gangs; the issue is opening doors that might otherwise remain closed, of giving a young one time for finding a purpose in life.

So we come to the adult, responsible for his or her own life (supposedly), and allegedly a free and articulate member of society. What possibilities of solitude are available even to the adult family member, husband, or wife? The worker, blue-collar or white-collar, has few exits in life through which the imagination can escape. As we have seen, the life of the city and the suburb, the demands of neighbors and churches, take over the week and invade the weekend.

This is hard, particularly for women. I can recollect my own mother fighting for space and time. Most of them lose the battle. Give them "rooms of their own."

A society therefore that protected and honored the inner life would have to permit (horror of horrors, to some!) a certain amount of paid idleness, as well as provide work for its members. I have seen statistics that suggest that in spite of the rising productivity of the American worker, she or he is working the same hours that she or he did twenty years ago, if not more. (I am speaking of paid work; unpaid work inside the home is still work). One would think that it would be possible to diminish the number of hours in the working day without layoffs or pay cuts, but anyone who thinks that must have been living in a broom closet — the only place where the words "speed up" are never uttered nor heard.

And still we hear demands for more productivity and denunciations of "welfare chiselers." Whether everyone given additional annual leave would use it wisely, is aside from the point: to waste free time, one must have free time. And again, the women are the ones who are going to have the hardest time getting it.

People should be turned loose. It isn't just students who should have a *Wanderjahr*, or professors who deserve a sabbatical. Money should be found to permit Mother to finish her novel, if it takes a year to do it. This should be set up on a cooperative basis, like an insurance policy; as we join in covering each others' risks, we should be joining to help people take the time off to build boats or learn Spanish. Having to make an investment might discourage the wastrel or the con artist (although these are so prevalent that we cannot expect them to be entirely eliminated; having elections does not automatically prevent corruption in government).

Probably the loneliest American among our familiar

heroes was Abraham Lincoln. This was not simply the result of the strain of being president during the nation's worst and most devastating war; he probably suffered from Marfan's syndrome, which would have taken his life even if the assassin's bullet had not. His vivid dreams and sense of the ominous make him one of America's solitaries, even if he was under the spotlight for five terrible years. While everybody knows about Lincoln, and most admire him, few would care to drain his cup.

A society that honored the inner life would have to re-evaluate the status of values we now associate with suburbia and the family. Families would still exist; they exist among the primates and many other animals; but the person who chose to remain single would have to be considered as one variation of the normal; single would no longer be considered singular. The artist would be as acceptable as the householder; the solitary might be a Buddha. Bugs Bunny would be as valued as Elmer Fudd: it takes both kinds to make a society.

Another requirement for the fostering of the inner life would be the development of a new view of religion. It's easy enough to criticize the hierarchical religions, with their bishops and disciplines; and easier yet to attack fundamentalists, whether as a tendency within the familiar churches or as founders of self-destructive cults. A shiftier target is the constellation of New Age religions, which — some of them — foster, or seem to foster, the very inner life we are endeavoring to protect. The difference among these various New Age groups, and between them and the kind of religious body we are searching for, could be described in terms of their emphasis: between the development of the soul and the development of the self. The soul seeks union with higher Powers, however described or guessed at. The self wants to "feel good," to be in balance, to attain health, harmonious living, the love of one's peers. The soul is prepared to be tried in fire. The self hopes to avoid indigestion by eating bamboo shoots. The soul hopes all things, believes all things, endures all things. The self wants them right here and now. The soul wrestles with its Deity. The self "blisses out." The soul speaks to that of God in every body. The self thinks that the body is God. The soul believes in self-mastery. The self believes in that amusing, but vulgar, creature of the cartoonist Robert Crumb, "Mr. Natural." *Anathema maranatha.*

Any religion, therefore, that fostered the inner life would have to revive that figure of fun — as we see him now — the hermit. Hermits were "athletes of God," not merely eccentrics, and while the possibility of real solitude is now very limited, in a world of nearly six billion people, most of the churches have retreats, and nearly all of them foster periods of silence and withdrawal. Helen

Waddell's book, *The Desert Fathers* (1936) gives a good account of the early hermits in their own words, and describes their discovery of eternity. Native Americans, too, have a period of withdrawal and fasting, sometimes providing the contemplative with a new name or perhaps a guardian spirit. The Zen Buddhist and Taoist traditions are full of hermits and solitaries, "immortals" of disreputable appearance, but filled with laughter, herbal wisdom, and gnomic remarks.

The silence of late Christmas Eve,
when all the revelers are asleep.

The real enemy of the inner life is not service, but "infotainment," distraction, the accumulation of trivia (can you visualize the inner life of the people who memorize fifty years of baseball statistics?) as well as the "nannyism" of modern life, the intrusion, by mail, telephone, or personal contact, of all those who want to waste your time, spend your money, and dictate your opinions. From this point of view the hermit and the worker are on the same side: unexpected revolutionary comrades-in-arms.

How to Get There from Here

By its very nature the society friendly to the inner life cannot be brought about by war or legislation — the two ways of "getting things done" in the twentieth century. The way thither will be found by individuals working in concert, but without formal organization; not necessarily "dropping out" completely, but simply by refusing to bother with watching television, answering all e-mail, or attending public meetings.

The first of these is through love. Our culture is so supersaturated with calls for love that this remark must seem sentimental or otiose, but the love I am talking about is the kind defined by Eric Fromm in his Art of Loving (1956) in these words: "Love is the active concern for the life and growth of that which we love" (italics his). The person who, presented with your magnum opus, thirty years in the making, skims the introduction and then misplaces the volume, does not love you, whatever he may urge to the contrary.

Back in 1936 Sherwood Anderson, in a letter to Theodore Dreiser, propounded a scheme whereby every writer or artist would sit down and write a colleague a letter of respect, admiration, and encouragement. This task each writer would perform every morning, choosing a different fellow worker each time, so that the late morning or afternoon mail would include, along with bills and rejection slips, a brief note telling the poet or novelist how good some fellow craftsman thought him. Of course the scheme never got off the ground, since most real writers are not terribly interested in each other's work, save as a tree to rub their bearlike backs against; but there should be someone in each artist's life who really cares about that artist's work, whether the caring is done by spouse, lover, or professional colleague.

The pathway to the good society takes the road of mutual interest in the work and personal growth of others. She will love you if you care about her doctoral thesis, or her household work.

The necessity of turning people loose, for a while, from the daily grind, even if they are involved in the world of work, requires funding — and the spirit of generosity that makes some such funding possible. Of course all countries have quarrels over budgets, but my point is this: No such support, public or private, is possible unless *the right to be different* is accepted, nay accentuated. The idea that the conservative taxpayer, or wealthy donor, should have the veto over all that is "rich or strange" would have to be abandoned. Again, it should be just as possible to get time off to build a boat as to paint a picture. Freedom should not only be granted; it should be supported with grants. Freedom to die, exhausted and frustrated, is no freedom at all.

A great deal of value should be placed on solitude and silence. "Leave him alone; he's got a right" to be by himself, or herself, should be part of the human vocabulary. Nobody should have to suffer unwanted phone calls during a print run, while the pots are in the kiln, or while cooking for a hungry family. At the very least, a "do not disturb" signal should be standard equipment on every telephone sold. Also, a period of retreat should be available to everyone, in every household, as a time-honored custom.

The destruction of American cities, and the consequent "white flight" to the suburbs, is regrettable but at this point irreversible. A busy editor I know, working out of her own home, has a sign on the door intended to discourage sales people, evangelists, and other flies on the body politic from distracting her while she gets out her magazine. Neighbors, too, will have to respect this separateness. Radios must be turned down. Television must be restricted to its den. Barking dogs must be silenced. Peace and quiet, mine and thine, must come first. Everything in our society that utilizes a captive audience should be strenuously opposed, at least in the case of free adults.

Conclusion

There really doesn't seem to be any way to provide for a society that honors the inner life except to insist on it.

The most important event in the known history of the universe was the appearance of the human mind. So far as I know, this event was unique. Then, if the brain is like other organs of the body, it must be subject to abuse, disease, and injury. If it is the source of thoughts and feelings, of the inner life, the mind deserves not only protection but careful cultivation. It needs love and contact with other minds, without which it will never develop language and civility. But the brain also needs the oxygen of solitude, without which it is likely to grow dull or even lose its harmony. It needs a window to stare out of, and to daydream. The political act of daydreaming is an act for the preservation of sanity.

From this reflective solitude comes, I suggest, the turning back to "the social droves," and the demands for freedom, justice, equality, and the other requirements for a decent life that sometimes in unity, sometimes in conflict with each other or with other human beings, make up the lone tale we call the history of the human world. How that story will turn out, we do not know. But the fact that we can think about the future, comes with our brainy human nature; and when we think on it, we are apt to daydream, with fear or hope, out the window.

"Silence, exile, and cunning" are the only paths to sanity, and only in a lonely but sane environment, at home, at work, or in the world, can that exquisite tulip, the inner life of the mind, the dream within the brain, flourish and blossom to the greater world's delight.

Now: put down this book, turn off the radio or television, and don't do anything: just gaze out the window — assuming you have one, and it doesn't look out on a prison yard or Jake's Auto Repair: (and if it does? you have been oppressed!) — let us hope you have at least a small garden.

Feel better? See? *SEE*?

Into the middle of the green
the mind, that runs up trees, pretends
the world starts, where the roofline ends,
then scrambles, to where blue is seen.

The mind's a squirrel: your ifs and buts
neglects for love-chasing in leaves;
strange opportunity it sees
to search for not-yet-opened nuts.

The leaves work harder than the mind.
They take light till the sun has set
and blue has turned to violet,
and Moon's a yellow lemon rind,

then rest. The mind delights to stray,
and, never finished with its streaming,
spends half the night in wastrel dreaming
from leaf to bole, from work to play.

A world's rogue flower is a mind,
In common life it strikes a root,
then blossoms hugely, to dispute
the power of seed of other kind;

then fades, then withers, then is seen
fallen and scattered, and will blow
the way the almond petals go,
into the middle of the green.

Acknowledgments

The author wishes to thank the following Friends, and friends, who have viewed this essay and made helpful comments:

Vashek and Claudette Cervinka, whose suggestions induced me to make extensive cuts and revisions; also Lauren Abell. These Friends belong to Davis (CA) Friends Meeting.

Dr. Whitney H. Gordon, Ball State University, Muncie, IN, an old friend, who put up with the eccentricities evident in the typescript.

Dr. Benjamin C. Hammett, clinical psychologist, who sent a collection of periodical articles, of which the emphasis is on isolation as therapy: useful background reading.

The poem given at the end of the essay is from the author's In the Dome of Saint Laurence Meteor (Oakland, CA, Regent Press, 1999). The poem scattered in italics through the essay, appears as "Alone/Solo," in the author's Sweetwater Ranch (Regent Press, 2002). Both are reprinted by permission of the publisher.

For Further Reading

Besides the authors and titles cited in the text, the following books may help illuminate this difficult subject:

Bruner, Jerome S. On Knowing: Essays for the Left Hand. Atheneum, 1962.

Dillard, Annie. Holy the Firm. Harper & Row, 1977.

Grumbach, Doris. Fifty Days of Solitude. Beacon Press, 1994.

Hirshfield, Jane. Nine Gates: Entering the Mind of Poetry; Essays. HarperCollins, 1997.

Milosz, Czeslaw. A Book of Luminous *Things; An International Anthology of Poetry, Edited with an Introduction*. Harcourt Brace, 1996.

Peace Pilgrim, Her Life and Work in Her Own Words, Compiled by Some of Her Friends. An Ocean Tree Book, 1953.

Pieper, Josef. *Leisure the Basis of Culture*. Translated by Alexander Dru, with an introduction by T. S. Eliot.

Pantheon Books, 1952. Originally published in German as *Masse und Kult*, and *Was heisst Philosophieren?*

Zen Flesh, Zen Bones: A Collection of Zen and Pre-Zen Writings, compiled by Paul Reps. Anchor Books, 1961.

Many other books, such as Thoreau's *Walden*, can be found under the Library of Congress subject heading SOLITUDE, in any academic or public library.

About the Author

Noel Peattie was born in 1932. He earned degrees in philosophy from Pomona College and Yale University, and a Masters in Library Science from UC Berkeley. Entering the library profession, he published a newsletter for librarians and others interested in the small press and dissident literature, as well as a novel, five books of poems, and (with the late John C. Swan) a book on freedom of speech versus social responsibility. He has been Librarian to the Davis Friends Meeting in California since 1973.